ENCHANTED ISLANDS

Voices and Visions from the Caribbean

A Journal

Conceived and compiled by Maxine Rose Schur

POMEGRANATE ARTBOOKS ✸ SAN FRANCISCO

Front cover: Mario Carreño (Cuban, b. 1913). *Exorcism on the Lake*, 1989.
Oil on canvas, 51 x 51 in. Collection of Patricio Garcia F., Chile.

Published by Pomegranate Artbooks
Box 6099, Rohnert Park, California 94927

ISBN 0-87654-076-0
Catalog No. A825

Pomegranate publishes several other illustrated journals as well as books,
address books, calendars, notecards, posters, bookmarks, and postcards.
For information on our full range of publications, please write to
Pomegranate, Box 6099, Rohnert Park, California 94927.

Designed by Tim Lewis
Printed in Korea

*L*ying at the junction of destination and dream, the Caribbean islands are much visited and little understood. Tourists enthralled by island life are often unaware of island lives. Yet, rich cultures have flourished for centuries in the scattered countries of the Caribbean, creating distinct societies as well as a pan-Caribbean aesthetic. Though each island is unique, they have historical connections: the experiences of colonialism and slavery, the influence of Christianity, a legacy of aboriginal mythology, and an affinity with African motifs.

On limited land but with boundless dreams, people of the Caribbean first communicated their histories orally. In the voodoo chants of Haiti, in the call-and-response work songs of Jamaica, and in the decima lyrics of Puerto Rico, people's lives were told and retold. Through the fortunes of war, languages changed back and forth, nurturing new ones such as Creole and Papiamento that added island rhythm to speech.

This journal reflects today's Caribbean diversity by presenting both the words and images from some of the foremost writers and artists of the region. The poignant reflections of Trinidad's Senya Darklight; the powerful images of Jamaica's Daisy Myrie; the playful, sensual poetry of Haiti's Emile Roumer—all are part of the lively mixture of literature collected for this journal, a veritable Caribbean gumbo of sensibilities and styles.

The paintings, too, vary in style, but all are animated by the love for color and light that comes from living with sun and sea. And like much of the writing, each painting evokes what Cuban poet Alejo Carpentier called "magic realism"—an enchanted way of seeing that transcends everyday reality. From the Renaissance-style vision of Puerto Rico's Rafael Trelles to the celestial landscape of Haiti's Jean Louis Senatus, this is art that amazes the eye, showing us how often in pictures, as in words, beauty comes on the wings of surprise.

MAXINE ROSE SCHUR

ANDRE NORMIL (HAITI). *PARADISE*, 1990. OIL ON CANVAS, 20 X 30 IN.
COLLECTION OF GALERIE MACONDO, PITTSBURGH, PENNSYLVANIA.

At the beginning of beginnings,
there was a woman and a man
like you and me. The first spring flowed at their feet,
and the woman and the man
entered the spring and bathed in life.

—Jacques Roumain (Haiti)

Our Caribbean / a bandolier
of emerald isles / circling
the waist / of twin continents
suspended miraculously
between Atlantic deeps
and the sun . . .

—Jan Carew (Guyana)

Love for an island
is the sternest passion:
pulsing beyond the blood
through roots and loam
it overflows the
boundary of bedrooms
and courses past the
fragile wall of homes . . .
—**Phyllis Allfrey (Dominica)**

EMILCAR SIMIL (HAITI, B. 1944) *UNTITLED*, 1986.
OIL ON CANVAS. COLLECTION MICHEL AND TONI MONNIN, PETIONVILLE, HAITI.

Say, is my skin beautiful?
Soft as velvet,
As deep as the blackness of a weeping night.

—**George Campbell (Jamaica)**

Honey, pepper, leaf-green limes,
Pagan fruit whose
names are rhymes,
Mangoes, breadfruit, ginger roots,
Grandillas, bamboo shoots,
Cho-cho ackees, tangerines,
Lemons, purple Congo beans.

—Agnes Maxwell-Hall (Jamaica)

J. PHILEMON (HAITI). *FRUIT TREE*, 1988.
OIL ON CANVAS, 24 X 16 IN. COLLECTION OF SHIRLEY BROOKS.

Everywhere plant life is sumptuous, luxuriant, encroaching, imperious. Vegetation reigns supreme. A power, an ardor bursts forth from all directions. All species meet face to face in the general advance up toward light.

—**Gilbert de Chambertrand (Guadeloupe)**,
from "Vacation at Monte Bello"

*The rain falls like knives
on the kitchen floor.
The sky's heavy drawer
was pulled out too suddenly.
The raw season is on us.*
—Derek Walcott (St. Lucia)

SUNDIATA WINSTON STEWART (BARBADOS, B. 1950). *TWO FRIENDS*, 1987.
MIXED MEDIA, 18 X 12 IN.

It was a Sunday morning. No one was going to fetch wood or water or going to the field. This was the quiet time. Getting in the mood for the Sunday service.

—Erna Brodber (Jamaica), from "The Spirit Thief"

*Each sunrise becomes
an act of faith and
each awakening an
affirmation of the spirit.*
—Omar Torres (Cuba)

CLAUDE DAMBREVILLE (HAITI, B. 1934). *AT MARKET*, 1990.
OIL ON CANVAS, 30 X 50 IN. COLLECTION OF ADOLEY ADUNTON.

Down from the hills, they come
With swinging hips and steady stride
To feed the hungry Town
They stirred the steep dark land
To place within the growing seed.
And in the rain and sunshine
Tended the young green plants,
They bred, and dug and reaped.
And now, as Heaven has blessed their toil,
They come, bearing the fruits,
These hand-maids of the Soil,
Who bring full baskets down,
To feed the hungry Town.

—Daisy Myrie (Jamaica), "Marketwomen"

We are all flutes.
Through us God makes
eternal music.
Can you hear the sound?
—Senya Darklight (Trinidad)

CÁNDIDO BIDÓ (DOMINICAN REPUBLIC, B. 1936). *ADAM AND EVE*, 1987.
ACRYLIC ON CANVAS, 50 X 40 IN.

I hold the splendid daylight in my hands
Inwardly grateful for a lovely day.
Thank you life.
Daylight like a fan spread from my hands
Daylight like scarlet poinsettia
Daylight like yellow cassia flowers
Daylight like clean water
Daylight like green cacti
Daylight like sea sparkling with white horses
Daylight like tropic hills
Daylight like a sacrament in my hands.
Amen.

—George Campbell (Jamaica), "Litany"

LISA HENRY CHU FOON (TRINIDAD, B. 1947). *WOMAN-EARTH SPIRIT*, 1991.
ACRYLIC ON CANVAS, 18 X 14 IN.
COLLECTION OF CHARLOTTE ELIAS, PORT OF SPAIN, TRINIDAD.

To be a child, again.
To be reborn.
To love, again.
To smell fresh-cut sugar cane, again.
To kiss some hidden part of memory.
To wash myself in a West Indian river,
and be baptised, again.
To be me, again.
To be me.

—Sebastian Clarke (Trinidad),
from "Memory:Passion:Escape"

Flying Fish:
The winged part
of the flying fish
Is not required
in the dish.

—Frank Collymore (Barbados)

Jean-Louis Senatus (Haiti, b. 1949). *Village in the Clouds*, 1993.
Oil on canvas, 18 x 24 in.
Collection of Monnin Gallery, Petionville, Haiti.

One fancies, at moments, that the island does not rise out of the sea, but floats upon it; that it is held in place, not by the roots of the mountains, and deep miles of lava-wall below, but by the clouds which have caught it by the top, and will not let it go. Let that cloud but rise and vanish, and the whole beautiful thing will be cast adrift; ready to fetch away before the wind.

**—Charles Kingsley (English),
from "At Last, A Christmas in the West Indies"**

Evening . . .
Hour brushed blue by the
moon. It shivers like a
scarf wound round the
supple throat of a woman.
—Léon Laleau (Haiti)

DIONISIO BLANCO (DOMINICAN REPUBLIC, B. 1953). PEASANT'S ROMANCE, 1989.
ACRYLIC ON CANVAS, 40 X 30 IN.

High-yellow of my heart, with breasts like tangerines,
you taste better to me than eggplant stuffed with crab,
you are the tripe in my pepper pot,
the dumpling in my peas, my tea of aromatic herbs.
You are the corned beef whose customhouse is my heart,
my mush with syrup that trickles down my throat.
You are a steaming dish, mushrooms cooked with rice,
crisp potato fries, and little fish fried brown . . .
My hankering for love follows you wherever you go.
Your bottom is a basket full of fruits and meat.

—Emile Roumer (Haiti), "The Peasant Declares His Love"

Early Saturday morning
the market bus
is a moving farm
going into Kingston town.
—**Monica Gunning (Jamaica)**

AMOS FERGUSON (BAHAMAS, B. 1922). *HERE COME THE BRIDE*, 1984.
ENAMEL ON CARDBOARD, 36 X 30 IN. WADSWORTH ATHENEUM, HARTFORD, CONN.
THE ELLA GALLUP SUMNER AND MARY CATLIN SUMNER COLLECTION FUND.

Night enters like a great ship
and throws upon the water
its first star
as an anchor.

—Luis Palés Matos (Puerto Rico)

DEMI RODRIGUEZ (CUBA, B. 1955). *WHERE THE IDEAS COME FROM*, 1993.
ACRYLIC ON CANVAS, 84 X 38 IN.
M. GUTIERREZ FINE ARTS, INC., KEY BISCAYNE, FLORIDA.

I like to sit at my back door
and watch the world go by,
My heart is turned
to the earth below
My soul toward the sky.

—Peter Lake (Montserrat)

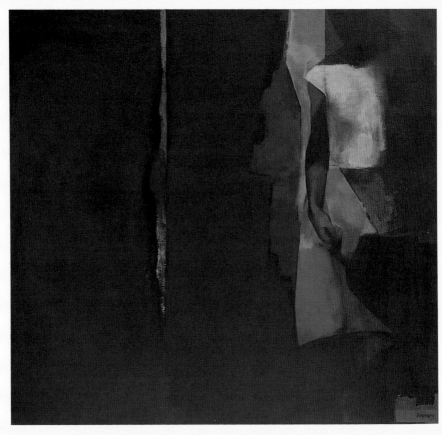

GEORGE RODNEY (JAMAICA, B. 1936). *FIGURE EMERGING*, 1974.
OIL ON CANVAS, 38 ¹/₄ X 40 IN. NATIONAL GALLERY OF JAMAICA, KINGSTON.

They don't even know
that I'm here.
They don't even feel
that I'm here.
They see me, but they don't see
me.
I'm here.

—Rudolph Kilzerman (Barbados), "The Invisible"

It is, here,
hungry
and in the dark,
that I make everything new.
—Pablo Armando Fernandez (Cuba)

CARLISLE A. HARRIS (TRINIDAD, B. 1945). *AMAITI, LOVE AND PITY*, 1992.
ACRYLIC ON CANVAS, 32 X 42 IN.

Love is not a grindstone
constantly grinding
wearing down to the bone

Love is not an interlocking
deadlock
of inseparable flesh
or a merging of metals
to smooth alloy

Love is a sunshawl
that keeps the beloved warm
Even the undeserving
love floods
risking all.

—Grace Nichols (Guyana), "Love"

*You curl your hair and paint
your face, not I;
I am curled by the wind,
painted by the sun.*
—Julia de Burgos (Puerto Rico)

FRANKLYN LATORTUE (HAITI, B. 1942.) *FÊTE PATRONAL*, 1965.
OIL ON CANVAS, 38 ½ X 50 IN. DAVENPORT MUSEUM OF ART, DAVENPORT, IOWA.

*Walking three miles
each Sunday morning
Nana goes to church
carrying her Sunday shoes
like a treasure*

*Walking barefoot
on hard rocky roads
the soles of her feet
cracked and toughened
wear better than leather.*

*Walking faster
she stubs her toe hard
Nana says, "Thank you, God,
it wan't me Sunday shoes."*

—Monica Gunning (Jamaica), "Walking to Church"

The weakness of most men
they don't know how
to become a stone or a tree.
—Aimé Cesaire (Martinique)

SHARON WILSON (BERMUDA, B. 1954). *TWO IN THE SHADE*, 1985.
PASTELS, 19 X 25 IN. © 1988 SHARON WILSON.

*When was the last time
we were quiet enough
to hear our hearts beating?*

—*Senya Darklight (Trinidad)*

The West Indies I behold
Like the Hesperides of old
Trees of life
with fruits of gold.
—James Montgomery, 1841

FRITZ ST. JEAN (HAITI, B. 1954). *AGOUE AND ERZOULE*, 1990.
OIL ON CANVAS, 24 X 32 IN.
COLLECTION OF GALERIE MACONDO, PITTSBURGH, PENNSYLVANIA

Oh, what stars they are, those
in that western tropical world!
How beautiful a woman
looks by their light,
how sweet the air smells,
how gloriously legible are the
constellations of the heavens.
—Anthony Trollope, 1859

TERESA GRIMES (GRAND CAYMAN, CAYMAN ISLANDS, B. 1952).
EAST END ROADSIDE, 1950. OIL, 25 X 33 IN.
COLLECTION CAYMAN ISLANDS GOVERNMENT, GOVERNOR'S MANSION, GRAND CAYMAN.

I awake to see sunlight streaming
Through the trees
Reflecting raindrops shimmering
In every color
Like millions of sparkling jewels
What a treasure
Right out in the open.

—Senya Darklight (Trinidad)

The night, charged with occult delights reveals phantoms and weaves spells . . .

—Jacqueline Bloncourt Hersalen

(Guadeloupe)

RAFAEL TRELLES (PUERTO RICO, B. 1957). *THE GARDEN OF THE POET II*, 1993.
OIL ON CANVAS, 24 X 34 IN. PRIVATE COLLECTION.

Our eyes are turquoise
Caribbean water.
Our hair is golden white
long stretches of
sandy beach.
—Diane Butler (St. Croix)

MILA JIMENEZ PREVIDI (PUERTO RICO, B. 1949). *AURORA I*, 1990.
OIL ON LINEN, 32 X 26 IN. COLLECTION OF LUIS CELA, SAN JUAN, PUERTO RICO.

Soon the sun
will give a big yawn
and open her eye
pushing the last bit of darkness
out of the sky.

—Grace Nichols (Guyana),
from "Early Country Village Morning"

At last to hold
a morning's breath,
To swell and feel
the rise of day!

—Alfredo E. Figueredo
(Cuba/St. Croix)

RAMON OVIEDO (DOMINICAN REPUBLIC, B. 1927). *ICE CONE VENDOR*, 1987.
MIXED TECHNIQUE, 40 X 30 IN.
COLLECTION OF CÁNDIDO GERÓN, SANTO DOMINGO, DOMINICAN REPUBLIC.

Open the door now
and watch from the verandah
the grey street where my father works

He has gone out among bicycle bells
gunfire of donkey carts
fishseller's cries . . .

                —Edward Kamau Brathwaite (Barbados), from "Clips"

I breathe and this garden
near the sea
breathes with me
the tree outside
stirs
with the rhythm
of my breathing.
—Herberto Padilla (Cuba)

Susan Alexander (Jamaica, b. 1929). *West End Weekend*, 1968.
Oil on canvas, 23 $^1/_2$ x 29 $^1/_2$ in. National Gallery of Jamaica, Kingston.

Jamaica . . .
it is a jewel
that smells like a flower.
—H. M. Tomlinson, 1912

MARLENE WELLINGTON GLASER (MONTSERRAT, B. 1956).
MOONLIT CARIBBEAN DREAM, 1992. WATERCOLOR, 22 X 16 ¼ IN.

The calm sea stretches without surf and without swell
It is an azure rug that unrolls itself
Swaying softly to the breath of a trade wind
Making iridescent reflections undulate . . .

—Damocles Vieux (Haiti), from "Marine"

There was a yelling of frogs;
and the insects were like an
invisible but ubiquitous
orchestra, incessantly engaged
in tuning up.

**—Aldous Huxley on Bridgetown,
Barbados, 1934**

JORGE ZENO (PUERTO RICO, B. 1948).
THE BIRTH OF THE MOON, 1992–1993. OIL ON CANVAS, 33 X 38 ¹/₂ IN.
GARY NADER FINE ART GALLERY, CORAL GABLES, MIAMI, FLORIDA.

I shall sit here and wait for the moon to rise,
And when she shall look at me,
From over the mountain-tops of tall bleak buildings
And come smiling down the valley of the streets,
I shall ask her here to sit with me
In a Chinese tea garden under a divi divi tree.

And a maiden golden like the moon shall come
Wearing a clean white apron . . .
And I shall show her a bright new sixpence
And bid her shut her eyes
And paint with the pigment of all her dreams
The broad brave canvas of the skies . . .

And she will think: "He is a little mad—
Decidedly he is a little mad." . . .

I shall sit here and wait for the moon to rise.

—Roger Mais (Jamaica), "I Shall Wait for the Moon to Rise"

It is sunset . . .
and there are
witchcrafts of color.
—Lafcadio Hearn

ROY LAWAETZ (ST. CROIX, U.S. VIRGIN ISLANDS, B. 1942).
CARIBBEAN FIGURES, 1993. ACRYLIC ON CANVAS, 32 X 42 IN.

A fantastic bestiary had arisen of dog-fish, oxen-fish, tiger-fish, snorer, blowers, flying fish; of striped, tattooed and tawny fish, fish with their mouths on top of their heads, or their gills in the middle of their stomachs . . . no forgetting the vieja-fish, the captain-fish, with its gleaming throat of golden scales; or the woman-fish—the mysterious and elusive manatees, glimpsed in the mouths of rivers where the saltwater mingled with the fresh, with their feminine profiles, and their siren's breasts, playing joyful nuptial pranks on one another in their water meadows.

—Alejo Carpentier (Cuba), from Explosion in the Cathedral

Ilan' life ain no funless ya treat
errybody like ya brudder,
ya sister, or ya frien'
Love ya neighbor, play ya part,
jes remember
das de art
For when ocean fence ya in,
all is kin.

—Susan J. Wallace (The Bahamas)

NICK QUIJANO (PUERTO RICO, B. 1953). *THE MERRY LIFE*, 1988.
GOUACHE ON PAPER, 22 ¹/₂ X 29 ³/₄ IN. PRIVATE COLLECTION.

Chiquín Molina, Chiquín Molina
Chiquín Molina Hué!
Where is the rhythm,
Caramba!
Of the mèrecumbe dance?
Hué!

—Puerto Rican folksong

Curacao: the long barren island, shaped like a ship hit broadside by a gale—it seems to be listing.
—Christopher Isherwood, 1949

COLIN GARLAND (JAMAICA, B. 1935). *IN THE BEAUTIFUL CARIBBEAN*, 1974.
LEFT PANEL OF TRIPTYCH, OIL ON CANVAS, 48 X 30 IN.
LENT BY THE ROYAL BANK OF JAMAICA LTD. COLLECTION.
ON PERMANENT LOAN TO THE NATIONAL GALLERY, KINGSTON, JAMAICA.

Like all who live on small islands,
I must always be remembering the sea,
Being always cognizant of her presence; viewing
Her through apertures in the foliage; hearing,
When the wind is from the south, her music, and smelling
The warm rankness of her; tasting
And feeling her kisses on bright, sunbathed days;
I must always be remembering the sea.

—Frank Collymore (Barbados), from "Hymn to the Sea"

I came from beyond the ocean
I drink water out of the sea
I lighten many a nation
And give myself to thee.
I am the sun.

—Jamaican riddle

MICHEL ST. VIL (HAITI, B. 1949). *MAGIC PASSAGE*, 1990. OIL ON CANVAS, 20 X 24 IN.
COLLECTION OF MONNIN GALLERY, PETIONVILLE, HAITI.

A chain of islands
have appeared where
none were
moments before . . .

　　　—**Senya Darklight (Trinidad)**

. . . grass dancing to the music
of the wind. I hear surf
in its shimmering song sound.
—Senya Darklight (Trinidad)

Mario Carreño (Cuba, b. 1913). *Exorcism on the Lake*, 1989.
Oil on canvas, 51 x 51 in. Collection of Patricio Garcia F., Santiago, Chile.

SOURCES

(in alphabetical order by author)

Excerpt from "Love for an Island," by Phyllis Allfrey, from *The Penguin Book of Caribbean Verse in English*, edited by Paula Burnett. London: Penguin Books Ltd., 1986.

Excerpt from "Clips," by Edward Kamau Brathwaite, from *Callaloo*, Vol. 11, No. 1. Baltimore, Md.: Johns Hopkins University Press, 1988.

Excerpt from "The Spirit Thief," by Erna Brodber, from *The Faber Book of Contemporary Caribbean Short Stories*, edited by Mervyn Morris. London: Faber and Faber, 1990.

Excerpt from the writings of Julia de Burgos from *Contemporary Women Authors of Latin America*, edited by Doris Meyer and Marguerite Fernandez Olmos. Brooklyn College Press, 1983.

Excerpt from "Us," by Diane Butler, from *Collage Two: Poets of St. Croix*, edited by Marty Campbell. St. Croix: 1991.

"Litany," by George Campbell, from *Caribbean Verse*, edited by O. R. Dathorne. London: Heinemann Educational Books Ltd., 1967.

Excerpt from "Our Home," by Jan Carew, from *The Penguin Book of Caribbean Verse in English*, edited by Paul Burnett. London: Penguin Books Ltd., 1986.

Excerpt from *Explosion in the Cathedral*, by Alejo Carpentier. London: Victor Gollancz Ltd., 1963.

Excerpt from "First Problem," by Aimé Cesaire, from *Miraculous Weapons*, translated by Clayton Eshelman and Denis Kelly, from *The Negritude Poets*, edited by Ellen Conroy Kennedy. New York: Thunder's Mouth Press, 1989.

Excerpt from "Vacation at Monte Bello," by Gilbert de Chambertrand, from *From the Green Antilles*, edited by Barbara Howes. New York: Macmillan and Company, 1966.

Excerpt from "Memory: Passion: Escape," by Sebastian Clarke, from *Breaklight*, edited by Andrew Salkey. New York: Doubleday, 1972.

"Hymn to the Sea," by Frank Collymore, from *Caribbean Verse*, edited by O. R. Dathorne. London: Heinemann Educational Books Ltd., 1967.

Excerpt from "Interlude," by Frank Collymore, from *Caribbean Voices*, Vol. 1, edited by John Figueroa. London: Evans Brothers Ltd., 1966.

"A chain of islands," "grass dancing to the music," "I awake to see sunlight streaming," "We are all flutes," and "When was the last time we were quiet," by Senya Darklight, from *Senya*, edited by Marty Campbell. Frederiksted, St. Croix, U.S. Virgin Islands, 1989.

Excerpt from "All Paths Are One," by Alfredo E. Figueredo, from *Collage Two: Poets of St. Croix*, edited by Marty Campbell. St. Croix: 1991.

"Walking to Church" and excerpt from "Jamaican Market Bus," by Monica Gunning, from *Not a Copper Penny in Me House: Poems from the Caribbean*. Honesdale, Penn.: Boyds Mill Press, 1993.

"The Invisible," by Rudolph Kilzerman, from *Breaklight*, edited by Andrew Salkey. New York: Doubleday, 1972.

Excerpt from "At Last, A Christmas in the West Indies," by Charles Kingsley, from *The Traveller's Dictionary of Quotations*, edited by Peter Yapp. London: Routledge and Kegan Paul Ltd., 1983.

Excerpt from "My Old Back Door," by Peter Lake, from *Dark Against the Sky: An Anthology of Poems and Short Stories from Montserrat*, edited by Howard Ferfus and Larry Rawdon. Montserrat: University of the West Indies School of Continuing Studies, 1990.

"I shall wait for the moon to rise," by Roger Mais, from *Caribbean Verse*, edited by O. R. Dathorne. London: Heinemann Educational Books Ltd., 1967.

Excerpt from "Impressionist Sketches," by Luis Palés Matos, from *Puerto Rican Poets*, edited by Alfredo Matilla. New York: Bantam Publishers, 1972.

Excerpt from "Jamaica Market," by Agnes Maxwell-Hall, from *3000 Years of Black Poetry*, edited by Alan Lomax and Raoul Abdul. New York: Dodd, Mead and Company, 1970.

"Marketwomen," by Daisy Myrie, from *Caribbean Voices*, Vol. 1, edited by John Figueroa. London: Evans Brothers Ltd., 1966.

Excerpt from "Early Country Village Morning," by Grace Nichols, from *Come on into my Tropical Garden*. London: A&C Black Publishers Ltd., 1988.

"Love," by Grace Nichols, from *Lazy Thoughts of a Lazy Woman*. London: Virago Press Ltd.

Excerpt from "Calm," by Herberto Padilla, from *Only Among Walkers*. New York: Farrar Straus Giroux, 1982.

"At the beginning of beginnings . . .," by Jacques Roumain, from *Sisters of the Dew*. New York: Reynal and Hitchcok, 1947.

"The Peasant Declares His Love," by Emile Roumer, translated by John Peale Bishop, from *The Negritude Poets*. New York: Thunder's Mouth Press, 1989.

Excerpt from "Against the Wind and the Sea," by Omar Torres, from *Carta de un Exilado*. Cuba: Tiempo Robado Ediciones, 1978.

Excerpt from "Marine," by Damocles Vieux, from *The Renaissance of Haitian Poetry*, edited by Naomi M. Garret. Paris: Presence Africaine.

Excerpt from "Another Life," by Derek Walcott, from *The Penguin Book of Caribbean Verse in English*, edited by Paul Burnett. London: Penguin Books Ltd., 1986.

"Ilan' Life," by Susan J. Wallace, from *Caribbean Canvas*, by Frané Lessac. New York: J. B. Lippincott, 1987.